AF604222
5 INGREDIENTS
Camping

THE AUSTRALIAN
Women's Weekly

# 5 INGREDIENTS *Camping*

# CONTENTS

# Introduction to CAMPING

With all the comforts of home, why even go camping at all? Trading your warm bed for the outdoors may seem ludicrous to some, but camping is all about enjoying the simplicity of less. We get to step back, take a big breath, and relax away from it all.

## NATIONAL PARKS

There are thousand of national parks across Australia. Many allow camping, although they may charge a small fee for use. Campsites will be basic but clean, with most offering limited facilities such as toilets or barbecues. Prices vary depending on the facilities the park has, it's location, and the season.

## FIRE RISKS

It is vitally important to know about bush fire safety when camping. Pay attention to fire danger warnings in your area, and check if there is a total fire ban before starting a campfire. Always extinguish your campfire correctly with water, ensuring that the entire fire is cool to the touch and well doused in water before you leave your campsite.

## BUSHWALKING

Most tracks in Australia are graded according to their difficulty. Those higher than a grade 2 (easy, level tracks) are more challenging, and may have serious accessibility issues. Make sure you wear sturdy boots, carry enough water, have a first-aid kit and if walking alone, ensure that someone knows where you are going and checks on you when you return. And never forget your sunscreen.

## CAMP FOOD

Whatever your camping plans, the first things to think about are how much space will you have, how are you going to keep food cold and fresh, and what will be the cooking source? Plan meals and equipment accordingly. Less is best.

Don't take your best pans, especially when cooking over a fire. Check out camping supply stores or second-hand stores for good cast-iron pans or light pots that are easy to carry. While a camp oven is not absolutely necessary, if you're going to be doing a lot of camping and if you're mostly cooking over an open fire, you will find a camp oven is versatile to cook a roast dinner, crusty damper or a winter pudding. Follow the instructions to clean and care for your cast-iron pan or camp oven and it will serve you for many years. It's a good idea to buy a lid-lifter as well.

## COOKING OPTIONS

• Gas stoves and camping rings are quick, clean and easy to use.

• Open fires are a more exciting cooking option and sitting around a campfire at the end of the day is the epitome of relaxation. The drawbacks are the weather, fire bans and the time it takes to let the fire die down to glowing embers for cooking (about 1-1½ hours). It's good to have a back-up gas option if you're planning on using a campfire. Scavenged wood can be used to build a fire – you will need several kilograms to make a fire to last a couple of hours.

• Another easy fuel source to use is chemical-free smokeless natural wood charcoal. It's light to carry, easy to light and is ready in about 30 minutes. You can move the pieces around with long tongs and it's less messy than wood.

• It's best to have some dry bricks or large pieces of wood to elevate the pan or camp oven over the embers, or a tripod to hang a camp oven from. It's very important not to use wet bricks or stones as they can explode when heated. Use the embers to add more heat when needed, or to pile on top of a camp oven lid.

• Make sure the fire is completely extinguished when finished. The ground will remain very hot for many hours afterwards so make certain the area is confined.

## REDUCE WASTE

• We've used whole cans and packets where possible to avoid leftovers.

• Oil from jars of char-grilled vegetables can be used for salad dressings or frying.

• Buy small packs of ingredients so you can use it all.

• Remove all your rubbish when you leave.

Australia is one of the most ecologically diverse countries in the world. Whether you long for the beauty of the ocean, the enveloping shade of the Northern rainforests, or the bright red of the interior, there is adventure waiting for you just around the corner.

# Campsites in AUSTRALIA

## WESTERN AUSTRALIA

### Osprey Bay

Osprey Bay is a medium-size campground off the Ningaloo Marine Park, located in the Cape Range National Park. Take a kayak and snorkel on the reef, a slice of paradise local's call 'the aquarium'. You are guaranteed to see the abundant sealife that lives beneath the waves. If you visit between late March–June, you might even be lucky enough to swim with a whale shark.

## SOUTH AUSTRALIA

### Ikara-Flinders Ranges National Park

At over 95,000 hectares, the Ikara-Flinders Ranges National Park is one of the oldest terrains in Australia. With its expansive semi-arid environment, the park is one of South Australia's most iconic destinations, rich with native wildlife, Indigenous heritage and impressive geological features. The range of activities available include bushwalking, four-wheel driving, bird-watching, and mountain biking.

The central hub of the national park is Wilpena Pound, accessed by a sealed road, but there are some parts of the national park that can only be accessed by dirt roads, of varying conditions.

## NORTHERN TERRITORY

**Ayers Rock Campground**

Uluru, sacred to the Indigenous Pitjantjatjara Anangu people, has captivated and awed visitors for thousands of years. While it's forbidden to camp in the ground of the Uluru-Kata Tjuta National Park itself, Ayers Rock Campground is only a 10-minute drive from Uluru, making it the perfect homebase to explore the national park.

The campground is open to motorhomes, caravans, cars and tents, and also has cabins available to rent. Take in the majesty of the great Red Centre and experience its peaceful presence.

## QUEENSLAND

**Cape Tribulation**

Situated in tropical Northern Queensland, the Daintree Rainforest is one of the oldest rainforests in the world. Cape Tribulation, nestled in between the rainforest and breathtaking Myall Beach, provides the perfect camping spot to explore both the beauty of the forest and the natural wonder that is the Great Barrier Reef. This is the only place in the world where two World Heritage areas meet.

## TASMANIA

**Cradle Mountain**

Dramatic peaks and glacial lakes define Cradle Mountain-Lake St Clair National Park. It's home to the Overland Track, a six day 65 kilometre walk, from which you can climb to the peak of the tallest mountain in Tasmania, Mount Ossa. Along the way there are huts and tent platforms to make life easier at the end of a long day of walking.

## NEW SOUTH WALES

**Cockatoo Island**

Why not try some urban camping for something different? Located in the middle of the world-renowned Sydney Habour, this camping experience might be best described as 'glamping'. There are a range of options available, from a simple tent to a more up-scale waterfront package. You can even elect to use a pre-erected tent. Originally a penal colony for convicts who had re-offended, Cockatoo Island today is a UNESCO World heritage site and a living museum to Sydney's maritime past.

## VICTORIA

**Alpine National Park**

Australian alpine parks are some of the most unique in the world. Here you can conquer Victoria's highest peak, Mt Bogong, bike across expansive mountain bike trails, white-water raft down thunderous rivers and in winter, cross-country ski through snow gum forests.

The park boasts the rugged The Falls to Hotham Trek, a three-day hike that crosses grassy plains, rocky summits and snow gum woodlands, with majestic views and unforgettable scenery.

1 **STAINLESS STEEL BARBECUE** choose a compact fold-up style

2 **KETTLE** for boiling water or brewing tea over a camp stove

3 **COFFEE POT**

4 **CAST-IRON POT** or camp oven for damper, stews and more

5 **ULTRA LIGHT STOVE** suitable for individuals and bushwalking

6 **RIDGED CHARGRILL PAN** choose a cast iron version

7 **CAMFIRE TOASTER** cook up to six slices of bread at once

8 **CHOPPING BOARDS** wood or plastic for chopping and serving

9 **SWISS ARMY KNIFE**

10 **CAMPFIRE GRILL** place over a wood or charcoal fire for cooking

11 **CAST-IRON FRYING PANS** heavy duty cookware

12 **SINGLE BURNER BUTANE STOVE** light and highly portable

13 **DOUBLE JUMBO JAFFLE IRON** for toasties and pies

14 **CANVAS TARP** protects your food against the elements

15 **TOOLS** tongs, extension fork and citrus press

16 **STURDY CONTAINERS**

17 **FIRESTARTERS & MATCHES**

18 **HEAT RESISTANT GLOVES**

# KITCHEN STAPLES

1 **COOKING OIL** spray oil, olive and vegetable oil

2 **CHILLI SAUCE** sriracha and sweet chilli sauce liven up meals

3 **SOY SAUCE** use as a seasoner, marinade or condiment

4 **SALT** flakes or table salt

5 **SUGARS** use brown or caster for drinks, marinades and baking

6 **PEPPER** use a mill or pre-ground for seasoning

7 **LONG-LIFE DAIRY** easy to store and carry milk and cream

8 **TEA & COFFEE**

9 **EGGS** the perfect instant breakfast, meal or snack

10 **SPICES** ground cinnamon, mixed dried herbs, cumin and smoked paprika

11 **HONEY & MAPLE SYRUP** for baking, marinades and dressings

12 **VINEGARS** apple cider, white wine, red wine and balsamic

13 **FLOURS** plain and self-raising

14 **GARLIC & ONIONS**

15 **STOCK CUBES** chicken, beef and vegetable

16 **BUTTER** we use unsalted butter in our recipes

17 **SAUCES & CONDIMENTS** ketchup, barbecue sauce, mustard, mayonnaise

# PANTRY STAPLES

# CAMP BREAKFAST

# CRISP CHEESY EGG 'TACOS'

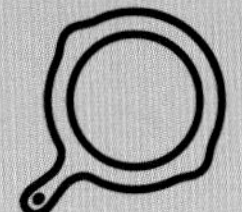

RECIPE SERVES 4

PREP & COOK TIME 15 MINS

IN THE SKILLET

## FIVE INGREDIENTS

2 cups (240g) grated cheddar

1 medium avocado (250g), chopped

200g tomato medley mix, chopped

## STAPLES

4 eggs

sauce of your choice, to serve

1 Heat a medium non-stick frying pan or skillet over medium-high heat. Sprinkle a quarter of the cheddar evenly over the base of the pan in a 12cm round; cook for 1 minute or until cheese just starts to melt.

2 Crack an egg into the centre of the cheese; cook for 2 minutes or until the white is set, the yolk remains runny, and cheese is crisp and browned. (If you prefer a more set yolk, cover the pan with a lid and cook 30-60 seconds longer.)

3 Slide the cheesy egg onto a plate, fold immediately in half to form a taco. Repeat with remaining cheese and eggs. Serve 'tacos' filled with avocado, tomatoes and the sauce of your choice.

# SKILLET BLUEBERRY HOTCAKE

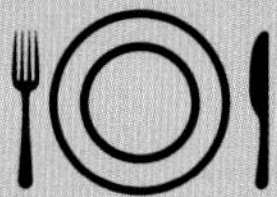

RECIPE SERVES 4

PREP & COOK TIME 30 MINS

IN THE SKILLET

### FIVE INGREDIENTS

325g bottle pancake mix

415g can blueberries in syrup

custard (optional), to serve

### STAPLES

1 tbsp oil of choice

1 Prepare a fire to glowing coals.

2 Heat a large cast-iron flat plate or skillet over the fire for 10 minutes or until very hot.

3 Meanwhile, prepare pancake mix according to packet instructions.

4 Add oil to the pan; swirl to grease the base and side. Pour in all the pancake mix; cook, covered, for 7 minutes or until set and the base is golden.

5 Remove pan from the heat; use a spatula to loosen the pancake from the base, then slide pancake onto a chopping board or plate. Invert the pan carefully over pancake; flip over so pancake is back in the pan, cooked-side up. Cook for a further 7 minutes or until golden on both sides and cooked through.

6 Serve hotcake topped with drained blueberries and some of their syrup and custard, if you'd like.

# PORK & APPLE BREAKFAST MUFFINS

RECIPE SERVES 4

PREP & COOK TIME 30 MINS

IN THE SKILLET

## FIVE INGREDIENTS

- 6 thick pork sausages (500g)
- ¼ cup (110g) caramelised onion relish
- 410g can pink lady apple slices in juice, drained
- 4 breakfast muffins, split in half horizontally
- 30g baby rocket leaves

## STAPLES

- 1 tbsp oil of choice
- 1 clove garlic, crushed

**1** Heat oil in a large frying pan or skillet over medium-high heat; cook sausages, turning occasionally, for 15 minutes or until browned and cooked through. Add 1 tablespoon of the onion relish to pan; turn sausages to coat.

**2** Push sausages to one side of the pan. Add apple and garlic to the pan; cook, stirring, for 2 minutes or until warmed through and golden. Season to taste. Transfer sausage and apple mixture to a plate. Cover to keep warm.

**3** Wipe pan clean and return to the heat. In batches, toast muffins for 1 minute each side.

**4** Cut sausages in half lengthways. Spread 2 teaspoons caramelised onion relish over each muffin base. Divide three sausage halves, apple and rocket among muffin bases. Season to taste. Sandwich with muffin tops.

Turn Knob clockwise to close.
IMPORTANT: Turn knob to the OFF position and raise the lever to UNLOCK after use.

# CHEAT'S PAIN SUISSE

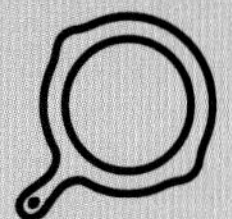

RECIPE MAKES 6

PREP & COOK TIME 20 MINS

IN THE SKILLET

## FIVE INGREDIENTS

1½ tbsp custard powder

6 mini hotdog brioche buns

¾ cup (250g) Nutella

## STAPLES

1 tbsp caster sugar

1½ cups (375ml) long-life milk

2 tsp butter or oil of choice

1 Whisk custard powder, sugar and milk in a large frying pan or skillet over medium heat; cook, stirring, for 5 minutes or until custard boils and thickens to a spreadable consistency.

2 Split buns horizontally, not quite cutting through to the other side. Spread brioche pockets with custard.

3 Place Nutella in a small cup or bowl; gradually stir in 1-2 tablespoons water to thin to a drizzling consistency.

4 Rinse and dry frying pan. Return pan to medium-high heat with butter or oil; once hot, add buns, in two batches. Cook for 1 minute each side or until lightly toasted.

5 Carefully open pain Suisse, drizzle Nutella on custard; sandwich together to serve.

***tip*** *You can also make the pain Suisse by inserting chocolate chips or a square of chocolate in the bun with the custard.*

# PESTO & HAM OMELETTES COOKED IN A BAG

RECIPE SERVES 4

PREP & COOK TIME 20 MINS

IN THE CAMP OVEN

## FIVE INGREDIENTS

- 8 slices ham (160g)
- ⅔ cup (180g) sundried tomato or basil pesto
- 1 medium red capsicum (200g), chopped finely
- 1 cup (120g) grated cheddar
- 2 green onions, sliced thinly

## STAPLES

- 8 eggs
- 2 tsp oil of choice
- sauce of choice, to serve (optional)

**1** Bring a large camp oven filled with water to a simmer. Finely chop half the ham.

**2** Place 2 eggs (cracked) and 1 tablespoon pesto into each snack-size zip-lock sandwich bag; press out the air and seal. Gently press each bag with the palm of your hand until the eggs and pesto are well combined.

**3** Open bags and evenly divide chopped ham, capsicum, cheddar and green onion among each. Gently press the bags to combine ingredients; press out the air and seal top.

**4** Place bags in the simmering water; cook for 12 minutes, turning halfway through, or until eggs are set. Open bags and carefully remove omelettes.

**5** Meanwhile, heat oil in a medium frying pan over medium-high heat. Cook remaining ham, turning for 5 minutes or until golden.

**6** Serve omelettes with fried ham, remaining pesto, and your sauce of choice.

***tips*** *You will need 4 snack-size zip-lock sandwich bags. Keep omelettes in the bag for a portable meal. Serve with toasted baguette, if you like.*

# FISHERMAN'S BREAKFAST

RECIPE SERVES 4

PREP & COOK TIME 10 MINS

IN THE SKILLET

### FIVE INGREDIENTS

4 white baps
500g short-cut bacon rashers
12 large scallops (300g)

### STAPLES

butter, to spread
2 tsp oil of choice
tomato or brown sauce, to serve

**1** Split rolls horizontally. Spread each roll generously with butter.

**2** Heat oil in a large frying pan over medium-high heat. Cook bacon, turning, for 5 minutes or until golden. Divide bacon among buttered rolls.

**3** Return frying pan to heat, cook scallops in the bacon fat for 1 minute on each side or until golden and just cooked through; divide among rolls. Serve buns with tomato or brown sauce.

***tips*** *You could also use prawns in place of scallops, if preferred. If you are a fan of chilli you can add a sprinkling of chilli flakes when cooking the bacon.*

# ISRAELI BREKKIE SANDWICH (SABBICH)

RECIPE SERVES 4

PREP & COOK TIME 25 MINS

ON THE GRILL

## FIVE INGREDIENTS

1 large eggplant (500g), sliced thickly

⅓ cup (80g) drained sliced pickled jalapeños, plus 1 tbsp pickling liquid

4 pitta breads (400g)

220g tub harissa hummus

60g baby spinach leaves

## STAPLES

2 tbsp extra virgin olive oil

sriracha or hot sauce (optional), to serve

1 Preheat a barbecue, grill plate or frying pan over medium heat. Combine oil and eggplant in a medium bowl; season to taste. Grill eggplant slices for 7 minutes each side or until charred and tender. Return eggplant to the bowl and drizzle with jalapeño pickling liquid.

2 Toast the pittas on barbecue for 1 minute each side. Carefully split open.

3 Spread hummus inside each pitta; divide eggplant, jalapeños and spinach evenly among pittas. Serve drizzled with sriracha or hot sauce, if you like.

***tips*** *You can also add sliced tomato or a hard-boiled egg to the pittas. For a no-cook version, swap fresh eggplant for the same weight of store-bought chargrilled eggplant and stuff into untoasted pittas.*

# FRENCH CRUMPETS WITH SMOKED SALMON

RECIPE SERVES 6

PREP & COOK TIME 30 MINS

IN THE SKILLET

## FIVE INGREDIENTS

- 200g green onion and chive cream cheese, softened
- 6 square crumpets (425g)
- 120g baby spinach leaves
- 250g sliced smoked salmon

## STAPLES

- 3 eggs
- ¼ cup (60ml) long-life milk
- 50g butter

**1** Prepare a fire to glowing coals.

**2** Heat a large cast-iron skillet over the fire for 5 minutes or until medium-hot.

**3** Meanwhile, whisk three-quarters of the cream cheese, the eggs and milk in a medium bowl until smooth and combined. Working with one crumpet at a time, dip into egg mixture, draining off excess.

**4** Add half the butter to the pan; swirl to grease the base. Add half the crumpets to the pan, cook for 3 minutes; turn and cook a further 2 minutes or until golden. Remove from pan. Repeat with remaining butter and crumpets.

**5** Add the spinach to pan; cook for 30 seconds or until just wilted.

**6** Serve crumpets topped with wilted spinach, a dollop of remaining cream cheese and the smoked salmon. Season.

# MUSHROOM CROQUE MADAME

RECIPE SERVES 4

PREP & COOK TIME 25 MINS

IN THE SKILLET

## FIVE INGREDIENTS

29g packet white sauce mix

50g gruyère cheese, grated coarsely

4 large field mushrooms (400g), stalks trimmed

250g thinly sliced shaved leg ham

50g baby spinach leaves or greens of choice

## STAPLES

1 cup (250ml) long-life milk

½ cup (125ml) oil of choice

4 eggs

1 Prepare white sauce mix with milk in a small saucepan according to stove-top packet instructions; stir through grated cheese until melted. Remove from heat; cover to keep warm.

2 Meamwhile, heat a large frying pan or skillet over medium heat. Add 2 tablespoons of the oil; cook mushrooms for 3 minutes each side or until golden and tender. Transfer to a plate, cover to keep warm.

3 Add 2 tablespoons oil to frying pan; cook ham, turning for 5 minutes or until golden. Transfer to plate. Add spinach to pan; cook for 30 seconds or until just wilted. Transfer to plate.

4 Heat remaining oil in fyring pan. Crack eggs into pan; cook for 4 minutes or until whites are set and yolks are cooked to your liking.

5 Arrange spinach then ham on mushrooms; top with a fried egg and drizzle with white sauce. Season to taste.

# EASY BREAKFAST SCALLION BREAD

RECIPE SERVES 8

PREP & COOK TIME
1 HOUR 30 MINS

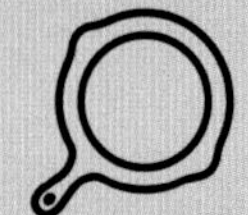

IN THE SKILLET

## FIVE INGREDIENTS

500g packet Lighthouse Pizza & Focaccia bread mix

⅓ cup (80ml) sesame oil

¼ cup (40g) sesame seeds

8 green onions, sliced thinly

¼ cup (60ml) chilli oil

## STAPLES

6 eggs

¼ cup (60ml) vegetable oil

**1** Place flour mixture and contents of yeast sachet into a large bowl. Add 1 cup (250ml) luke-warm water and the sesame oil; mix until the dough forms a ball. Knead for a further 5 minutes in the bowl or until smooth and elastic. Cover; set aside in a warm place for 30 minutes or until doubled in size.

**2** Sprinkle sesame seeds and green onion over dough; knead to combine.

**3** Cut the dough in half. Transfer one half to a piece of baking paper; gently stretch and press into a 1.5cm-thick, 30cm round. Carefully crack three eggs onto one half of the round; prick yolks with a fork to break. Fold the other half of the round over eggs and press edges to seal. Repeat with remaining dough and eggs.

**4** Heat a large cast-iron frying pan over medium heat on a camp stove for 5 minutes.

**5** Add 1½ tablespoons oil to pan. Carefully transfer one dough semi-circle into pan; cook for 6 minutes each side or until golden brown. Remove from pan and keep warm. Repeat with remaining oil and dough. Season to taste.

**6** Serve bread cut into wedges, drizzled with chilli oil.

# CORN CAKES

RECIPE MAKES
12 PANCAKES

PREP & COOK TIME 35 MINS

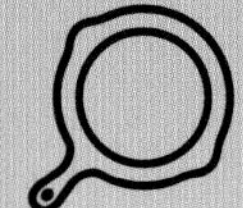

IN THE SKILLET

## FIVE INGREDIENTS

- 1½ cups (210g) Medjool dates, pitted, chopped coarsely
- 1½ cups (255g) instant polenta
- 535g box instant scone mix
- 5 small bananas (650g), halved lengthways

## STAPLES

- 250g butter, chopped
- 2 tsp table salt
- 2 eggs
- 2 cups (500ml) long-life milk
- 1 cup (250ml) olive oil
- ¼ cup (55g) caster sugar

1 To make the date butter, combine 200g butter, the dates and half the salt in a small bowl.

2 To make the batter, whisk polenta, scone mix, remaining salt, the eggs, milk and half the oil in a large bowl.

3 Heat 1 tablespoon of the remaining oil in a large cast-iron skillet or frying pan over medium heat. When oil is hot, pour three ½-cups of batter into the pan, spreading each into a 12cm round; cook for 2 minutes each side or until golden brown, adding more oil as required. Repeat three more times with remaining batter to make 12 pancakes in total. Cover to keep pancakes warm between each batch.

4 Heat remaining 50g butter in the skillet until butter is foaming. Place sugar on a plate and press cut-side of bananas into sugar. Add bananas, cut-side down to pan; cook for 3 minutes or until lightly golden. Turn and cook for 1 minute or until caramelised and warmed through.

5 Serve corn cakes topped with bananas and date butter.

# VANILLA STRAWBERRY PORRIDGE

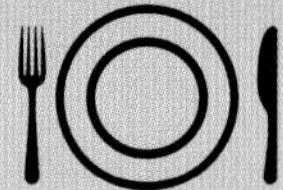

RECIPE SERVES 4

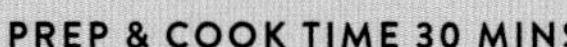

PREP & COOK TIME 30 MINS

IN THE CAMP OVEN

## FIVE INGREDIENTS

500g strawberries, hulled and sliced

2 tsp vanilla bean paste

2 cups (260g) 5-grain porridge mix

1 litre (4 cups) milk of choice

1 cup (140g) mixed nuts

## STAPLES

¼ cup (90g) honey or maple syrup, to taste

**1** Combine strawberries, vanilla bean paste and honey in a medium bowl. Set aside.

**2** Add porridge mix, 3 cups (750ml) of the milk and 2 cups (500ml) water to a camp oven or large saucepan. Heat over medium heat; cook, stirring frequently, for 15 minutes or until porridge is thick and creamy.

**3** Serve porridge topped with remaining milk, the vanilla strawberries and nuts.

# XO EGG CROISSANTS

RECIPE SERVES 4

PREP & COOK TIME 15 MINS

IN THE SKILLET

## FIVE INGREDIENTS

- 4 croissants (300g), split in half
- 100g small shiitake mushrooms
- ¼ cup (75g) XO sauce, plus oil to drizzle
- 2 green onions, sliced thinly diagonally
- 1 cup coriander leaves

## STAPLES

- 2 tbsp butter or oil of choice
- 8 eggs

**1** Heat a large non-stick frying pan or skillet over medium-high heat. Place croissants in the pan, cut-side down, for 1 minute or until toasted and golden; remove and set aside.

**2** Melt half the butter or heat half the oil in the pan. Cut any large mushrooms in half. Cook mushrooms, tossing occasionally, for 4 minutes or until tender. Season to taste. Transfer to a plate and keep warm. Reduce heat to medium.

**3** Lightly whisk eggs and XO sauce in a large bowl until combined. Melt remaining butter in pan. Add egg mixture, wait a few seconds, then using a wide spatula, gently scrape the set egg mixture along the base of the pan for 1-2 minutes or until eggs are still creamy and barely set.

**4** Fill croissants with scrambled eggs, mushrooms, green onion and coriander leaves. Drizzle with a little XO sauce oil to serve.

***tip*** *Any roll or type of bread can be used in place of croissants, if preferred.*

# GOOEY CHEESY POTATOES

RECIPE SERVES 4

PREP & COOK TIME 25 MINS

IN THE CAMP OVEN

## FIVE INGREDIENTS

1kg small red potatoes, halved

400g melting cheese, such as raclette, smoked cheddar, fontina or gruyère, grated

½ cup chopped flat-leaf parsley

20 cornichons (300g), halved lengthways (see tip)

## STAPLES

1 small red onion (100g), chopped finely

**1** Place potatoes and 2 cups (500ml) water in a 25cm camp oven or large cast-iron skillet pan. Season. Cover and bring to the boil over high heat. Cook for 10 minutes or until tender and water has almost evaporated, turning halfway through.

**2** Drain off any remaining water and stand to steam for 1 minute. Sprinkle over cheese and onion; cover and cook for 3 minutes or until cheese is melted.

**3** Serve potatoes topped with parsley and cornichons.

***tip*** *Cornichons are small sour gherkins, you can substitute with other pickled gherkins, if preferred.*

ON-THE-GO

# LUNCH & SNACKS

# BOMBAY SANDWICH

RECIPE SERVES 4

PREP & COOK TIME 15 MINS

IN THE SKILLET

## FIVE INGREDIENTS

300g packet microwave Bombay potatoes (see tips)

8 slices white bread

2 tbsp mango chutney or eggplant pickle

2 large tomatoes (440g), sliced

1 Lebanese cucumber (130g), sliced

## STAPLES

2 tbsp oil of choice

**1** Heat 1 tablespoon of the oil in a large frying pan or skillet over medium heat; cook Bombay potatoes, turning occasionally, for 3 minutes or until heated through. Transfer to a plate and keep warm.

**2** Wipe frying pan clean. Return to medium-high heat with half the remaining oil. Cook bread slices, in two batches, for 1 minute each side or until golden.

**3** Spread chutney evenly over four slices of bread; top with cucumber, tomato and potatoes. Sandwich together with remaining toasted bread. Serve warm.

***tips*** *Bombay potatoes are a spiced Indian potato dish available pre-prepared in pouches from supermarkets. You could also use canned beetroot slices if fresh vegetables are unavailable.*

# FELAFEL PIZZA

RECIPE SERVES 4

PREP & COOK TIME 45 MINS

IN THE SKILLET

## FIVE INGREDIENTS

200g small Swiss brown mushrooms, sliced thickly

200g packet felafel mix

½ cup (130g) pasta sauce

⅔ cup (160g) drained chargrilled capsicum strips

150g haloumi, sliced thinly

## STAPLES

2 tbsp oil of choice

1 medium red onion (170g), sliced thinly

2 cloves garlic, crushed

1 tsp mixed dried herbs

**1** Prepare a fire to glowing coals.

**2** Heat oil in a 23cm cast-iron skillet over medium-high heat; cook onion for 4 minutes or until softened. Stir in garlic, mushrooms and herbs; cook for 4 minutes or until mushrooms are golden. Season. Transfer to a plate.

**3** Meanwhile, prepare felafel mix according to packet instructions.

**4** Wipe pan clean then grease and line with baking paper. Press felafel mixture evenly into the base of the pan.

**5** Spread pasta sauce over felafel base; spoon mushroom mixture evenly over sauce. Top with capsicum strips and haloumi. Cook over the fire for 30 minutes or until felafel base is crisp and cheese is melted (take care that baking paper is tucked up in pan so it doesn't ignite).

**6** Cut felafel pizza into slices to serve.

# CORN & TUNA FRITTERS

RECIPE MAKES 16 FRITTERS

PREP & COOK TIME 25 MINS

IN THE SKILLET

## FIVE INGREDIENTS

- 325g bottle pancake mix
- 300g can corn kernels, drained
- 425g can Italian-style tuna in oil, drained
- 6 green onions, chopped coarsely
- 175g kale slaw kit with dressing

## STAPLES

- 2 cloves garlic, crushed
- ½ cup (125ml) oil of choice
- sweet chilli sauce, to serve

1 Prepare a fire to glowing coals.

2 Heat a large cast-iron skillet over the fire for 5 minutes or until medium hot.

3 Meanwhile, prepare pancake mix according to packet instructions, using 1½ cups (375ml) water. Pour mixture into a bowl; add corn, tuna, green onion and garlic. Season and stir to combine.

4 Add oil to pan. Working in batches, place four ¼-cups of batter into pan; cook for 3 minutes each side or until golden and cooked through. Repeat three more times with remaining batter to make 16 fritters in total.

5 Serve fritters warm or at room temperature with kale slaw and dressing, and sweet chilli sauce.

IMPORTANT

# CRISPY TOFU KATSU ROLLS

RECIPE SERVES 4

PREP & COOK TIME 20 MINS

IN THE SKILLET

## FIVE INGREDIENTS

1 cup (75g) panko (Japanese) breadcrumbs

450g firm tofu, cut into 6 x 1cm slices

200g packet coleslaw mix

4 brioche hamburger buns with sesame seeds, split

## STAPLES

⅓ cup (50g) plain flour

2 eggs

½ cup (125ml) oil of choice

½ cup (150g) mayonnaise

sriracha or hot sauce, to serve

1 Heat a large cast-iron skillet over medium heat.

2 Meanwhile, place flour in a shallow bowl; season. In another shallow bowl, lightly beat eggs. Place breadcrumbs in a third shallow bowl. Coat tofu in flour; dip in egg, allow excess to drain off, then coat in breadcrumbs.

3 Add oil to hot pan to heat (it will heat quickly). Cook crumbed tofu for 2 minutes each side or until golden. Remove with tongs or a slotted spoon; drain on paper towel.

4 Combine coleslaw mix and mayonnaise in a medium bowl. Divide coleslaw among bun bases; top with one or two pieces of tofu, a drizzle of sriracha and bun top.

tip *You could use 600g sliced chicken breast fillets instead of the firm tofu, if preferred.*

# PINTO BEAN & MOZZARELLA TORTAS

RECIPE SERVES 6

PREP & COOK TIME 30 MINS

IN THE SKILLET

## FIVEINGREDIENTS

- 4 x 420g cans Mexican bean mix, drained, rinsed
- ½ cup (60g) pickled sliced jalapeños, chopped finely, plus 2 tbsp jalapeño pickling liquid
- 6 Turkish bread rolls (540g), split in half horizontally
- 500g mozzarella, sliced or grated
- 200g bag tortilla chips

## STAPLES

- ¾ cup (180ml) olive oil
- 1 large red onion (200g), sliced thinly
- sauce of choice, to serve

1 To make torta filling, combine beans, chopped jalapeños, pickling liquid and the oil in a large bowl. Season to taste.

2 Divide bean mixture among bread roll bases, leaving a 3cm border. Top bean mixture with onion and mozzarella. Sandwich rolls together, pressing down firmly; wrap in foil.

3 Heat a large frying pan over medium heat; cook tortas, in batches, weighed down with another frying pan or saucepan, for 5 minutes each side or until golden brown, heated through and mozzarella is melted.

4 Cut tortas in half to serve. Accompany with tortilla chips, your choice of sauce and extra jalapeños, if you like.

# FIVE SPICE POPCORN CHICKEN

RECIPE SERVES 6

PREP & COOK TIME 30 MINS

IN THE SKILLET

## FIVE INGREDIENTS

1kg chicken thigh fillets, cut into 4cm pieces

2 tsp five spice powder

1½ cups (225g) tempura batter mix

1 long red chilli, sliced thinly

## STAPLES

1 tbsp light soy sauce

½ teaspoon caster sugar

1 egg white

vegetable oil, to shallow-fry

½ cup (150g) Japanese (Kewpie) mayonnaise

1 Place chicken in a large zip-lock sandwich bag with soy sauce, five spice, sugar and egg white. Seal bag, then shake to coat chicken. Set aside for 15 minutes to marinate.

2 Add 1cm deep oil to a large frying pan or skillet; heat over high heat.

3 Meanwhile, add tempura batter mix to chicken bag; shake vigorously and massage bag to coat chicken well.

4 When the oil is hot (see tip), carefully place one-third of the chicken into the pan; cook for 5 minutes on each size or until chicken is golden brown and cooked through. Transfer chicken to paper towel. Season to taste. Repeat with remaining chicken.

5 Scatter with chilli and serve with mayonnaise.

***tip*** *To check if the oil is hot enough, drop a tiny bit of batter into it – it should sizzle on contact but not burn.*

# BÁNH MÌ BAGUETTES

PREP TIME 10 MINS

NO COOK

## FIVE INGREDIENTS

- 1 cooked barbecue chicken (900g)
- 2 baguettes (600g)
- 120g baby cos leaves
- 2 green onions, cut into batons
- 1 cup Vietnamese shredded daikon and carrot pickles

## STAPLES

- sauce of choice, to serve

**1** Pull chicken meat from bones, discarding skin and bones, then tear into long shreds.

**2** Cut each baguette in half down the middle, without cutting all the way through.

**3** Divide cos leaves, chicken, green onion and pickles between baguettes. Cut each into two or three portions. Serve bánh mì drizzled with your choice of sauce.

***tips*** *You could use pre-grated carrot or coleslaw mix as an alternative to Vietnamese pickles. Vietnamese pickles are available from Asian grocers. We used Japanese mayonnaise and sriracha as our sauces of choice in our bánh mì.*

# MAPLE CINNAMON TRAIL MIX

RECIPE MAKES
3 CUPS

PREP & COOK TIME 10 MINS

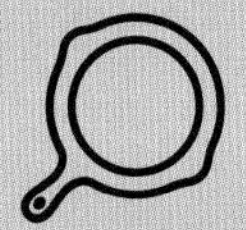

IN THE SKILLET

## FIVE INGREDIENTS

⅓ cup (80ml) maple syrup

1½ cups (250g) natural mixed nuts,

½ cup (75g) mixed dried fruit medley

1 tsp ground cinnamon

½ cup (35g) coconut flakes

## STAPLES

¼ tsp sea salt flakes

**1** Heat maple syrup and 2 teaspoons water in a medium skillet or saucepan over medium-high heat. Once bubbling, add remaining ingredients, except coconut flakes; stir continuously for 5 minutes or until well combined, maple syrup has evaporated and nuts are toasted. Stir in coconut flakes.

**2** Tip trail mix onto a greased tray and separate mixture; set aside to cool completely. Store in an airtight container for up to 1 month.

***tip*** *If you have some chilli flakes or chilli powder on hand add a little to your trail mix for a spice kick.*

# TACO POPCORN

RECIPE MAKES 16 CUPS

PREP & COOK TIME 15 MINS

IN THE CAMP OVEN

## FIVE INGREDIENTS

⅔ cup (160g) popping corn kernels

35g packet taco seasoning

50g finely grated Parmesan

100g yellow corn chips, broken coarsely

½ cup (150g) chipotle mayonnaise

## STAPLES

¼ cup (60ml) oil of choice

100g unsalted butter, chopped

**1** Heat oil in a large camp oven over medium-high heat. Once oil is hot, add corn kernels and cover with a tight-fitting lid. Cook, shaking pan occasionally, for 3-5 minutes or until popping sounds become infrequent. Transfer to a large bowl.

**2** Return pan to medium heat; melt butter. Stir in taco seasoning until well combined. Add Parmesan and stir quickly to melt. Working quickly, return popcorn to pan and stir to coat. Cover with lid and shake to cover popcorn in seasoning mixture. Add corn chips and shake to combine.

**3** Return popcorn to bowl and drizzle with chipotle mayonnaise to serve.

RED
SESSION ALE

# MINI CORN COB LOAF BAKED ROLLS

RECIPE MAKES 6

PREP & COOK TIME 35 MINS

IN THE CAMP OVEN

### FIVE INGREDIENTS

505g can chicken and corn soup

1½ cups (180g) grated cheddar

½ cup (120g) sour cream

6 green onions, sliced thinly

6 large round bread rolls (65g each)

### STAPLES

2 eggs, beaten lightly

1 Prepare a fire to glowing coals.

2 Combine soup, three-quarters of the cheddar, the sour cream, half the green onion and the eggs in a large bowl; season with salt and pepper.

3 Using a serrated knife, remove tops from bread rolls and reserve. Using a spoon, scoop out the soft bread from the rolls, leaving a 1cm-thick shell. Place hollow rolls in a camp oven fitted with a rack; divide soup mixture evenly into each roll. Sprinkle with remaining cheese and green onion.

4 Cover camp oven with lid and suspend 20cm above hot coals; cook for 25 minutes or until the filling is puffed and set. In the last 5 minutes of cooking time, add bread lids to the oven to warm and crisp.

# INDIAN-SPICED RICE, SMOKED SALMON & EGGS

RECIPE SERVES 4

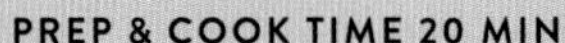

PREP & COOK TIME 20 MINS

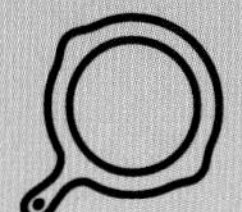

IN THE SKILLET

## FIVE INGREDIENTS

- 2 x 250g packets Indian-spiced basmati rice
- 200g green beans, halved lengthways
- 3 green onions, sliced thinly, white and green parts kept separate
- 2 x 150g hot smoked salmon fillets, skin removed, flaked
- 2 tbsp lemon juice

## STAPLES

- 2 tbsp olive oil
- 4 soft-boiled eggs, peeled, halved (see tip)

1 Heat oil in a large skillet or frying pan over medium heat; cook rice, beans and the white part of green onion for 6 minutes or until rice is warmed through and beans are tender. Season to taste.

2 Add flaked salmon and lemon juice to pan; stir until heated through.

3 Serve rice topped with eggs and remaining green onion.

***tip*** *For soft-boiled eggs, lower room temperature eggs carefully into a small saucepan of boiling water with enough water to cover. Boil for 6 minutes. Drain and peel.*

CENTRE

ESKY
portable ice box

# TUNA & ZUCCHINI FRYING PAN CAKE

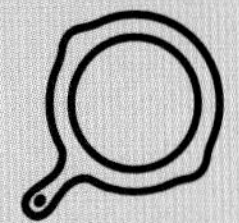

RECIPE SERVES 6

PREP & COOK TIME 35 MINS

IN THE SKILLET

## FIVE INGREDIENTS

56g packet cheese, broccoli and potato soup mix with croûtons

¾ cup (90g) grated cheddar

2 medium zucchini (240g), grated coarsely

2 x 125g cans tuna slices with chilli in oil

10 grape tomatoes, halved

## STAPLES

6 eggs

¾ cup (110g) self-raising flour

2 tbsp oil of choice

1 Whisk eggs and soup mix in a large bowl. Add flour, cheddar and oil; whisk until combined. Add zucchini; whisk until well combined. Season to taste (you won't need much salt due to the soup mix).

2 Drain tuna slices; reserve oil and chilli. Cut slices in half.

3 Grease a deep 23cm non-stick skillet or frying pan. Heat pan over medium heat. Working quickly, pour zucchini mixture into pan; arrange tuna and tomatoes on top.

4 Cover pan; cook, covered, for 15 minutes or until base is browned and mixture is almost set. Slide cake onto a plate or board. Invert pan over cake; flip. Cook cake for a further 5 minutes or until golden underneath.

5 Slide cake onto board. To serve, cut into wedges and drizzle with reserved tuna chilli oil.

***tip*** *You don't need to worry about squeezing out excess water from the zucchini as the soup mix acts as a thickener.*

# MONSTER CAMPFIRE COOKIE

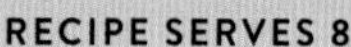

RECIPE SERVES 8

PREP & COOK TIME 55 MINS

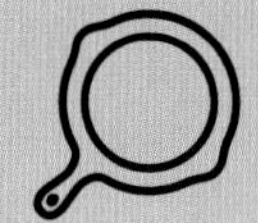

IN THE SKILLET

## FIVE INGREDIENTS

- ⅓ cup (75g) firmly packed brown sugar
- ½ tsp bicarbonate of soda
- 1 cup (130g) crunchy oat granola with berries
- ⅓ cup (65g) pepitas (pumpkin seed kernels)
- 180g dark chocolate, broken into squares

## STAPLES

- 125g butter
- ⅓ cup (75g) caster sugar
- 1 egg
- 1 tsp salt
- 1 cup (150g) plain flour

**1** Prepare a fire to glowing coals.

**2** Melt butter in a 28cm (top measurement), 22cm (base measurement) cast-iron skillet. Stir in sugars. Remove from heat; stand for 5 minutes.

**3** Stir in egg, then bicarb and salt. Stir in flour, in three batches, until combined. Add granola, pepitas and half the chocolate; stir to combine. Level the cookie surface.

**4** Cover pan with a heatproof lid or foil. Place on a flatplate over the fire. Cook for 30 minutes or until just firm. Gently press remaining chocolate into the top of the cookie.

**5** Serve warm or cooled, cut into wedges.

# SMOKED TUNA, BEAN & BEETROOT SALAD

RECIPE SERVES 4

PREP TIME 15 MINS

NO COOK

## FIVE INGREDIENTS

- 400g can 4-bean mix, drained
- 125g baby rocket leaves
- 2 x 125g smoked tuna slices in oil, drained
- 2 medium avocados (500g), peeled, sliced
- 250g packet cooked ready-to-eat baby beetroot, cut into wedges

## STAPLES

- ¼ cup (60ml) olive oil
- 1½ tbsp vinegar of choice

**1** To make the dressing, whisk oil and vinegar together in a small bowl. Season to taste. Add beans and toss to combine.

**2** Divide and arrange rocket, tuna, avocado, beetroot and dressed beans in four lunch boxes to go.

***tip*** *Smoked tuna can be substituted for any canned tuna or salmon of your choosing.*

# ITALIAN LUNCH BOX

RECIPE SERVES 2

PREP TIME 15 MINS

NO COOK

## FIVE INGREDIENTS

- 170g tub semi-dried tomatoes in oil
- 150g cured meat antipasto platter mix (see tips)
- 130g tub Deli Express mixed Mediterranean olives, drained
- 6 trimmed stalks celery (600g)
- 120g drained bocconcini

## STAPLES

- 1½ tbsp vinegar of choice
- 4 hard-boiled eggs (see tips)

**1** Reserve ¼ cup (60ml) semi-dried tomato oil in a small bowl, then drain tomatoes. Add vinegar of choice to oil; whisk to combine and season to taste. Divide dressing between two small containers.

**2** Between two lunch boxes to go, divide and arrange the cured meats, olives, drained semi-dried tomatoes, celery, hard-boiled eggs and bocconcini.

**3** Drizzle lunch boxes with dressing to serve. Accompany with bread, if you like.

***tips*** *We used a packet of mixed cured meats that includes prosciutto, soppressa and hot salami.*
*For hard-boiled eggs, lower room temperature eggs carefully into a small saucepan of boiling water with enough water to cover. Boil for 8 minutes. Drain.*

# AROUND THE FIRE
# DINNER

# GREEN CURRY COCONUT RICE WITH CHICKEN

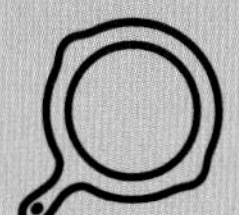

RECIPE SERVES 4

PREP & COOK TIME 55 MINS

IN THE SKILLET

## FIVE INGREDIENTS

600g chicken sausages

2 x 175g packets green curry meal base

1½ cups (300g) jasmine rice, rinsed

400ml can coconut milk

80g tube coriander paste

## STAPLES

1 tbsp oil of choice

1 medium onion (150g), chopped finely

2 cloves garlic, crushed

**1** Heat a large cast-iron skillet or camp oven over medium heat for 5 minutes or until hot.

**2** Meanwhile, squeeze mince from the sausage casings to make meatballs.

**3** Add oil to hot pan, then quickly add meatballs; cook, turning, for 3 minutes or until golden. Transfer to a plate. Add onion to pan; cook, stirring, for 3 minutes or until softened. Stir through garlic; cook for 30 seconds or until fragrant. Stir through green curry meal base, rice, coconut milk, coriander paste, browned meatballs and ½ cup (125ml) water.

**4** Cover with a lid; cook for 25 minutes or until liquid is absorbed and rice is cooked. Set aside, covered, for 5 minutes for rice to finish cooking.

***tips*** *If you have fish sauce on hand, stir through 1-2 tablespoons to taste. Line the pan with 2 sheets of baking paper in opposite directions to prevent rice from catching on the base of the pan and to assist with clean up. You can add Asian greens to the top of the rice during the last 5 minutes of cooking, if you like.*

Seductively Beer.

# CHEESY GOODNESS PUMPKIN GNOCCHI BAKE

RECIPE SERVES 4

PREP & COOK TIME 55 MINS

IN THE SKILLET

## FIVE INGREDIENTS

- 400g packet pumpkin gnocchi
- 505g can pumpkin soup
- 300ml thickened cream
- 1¼ cups (125g) finely grated Parmesan
- 400g packet garlic bread

## STAPLES

- 2 eggs
- 2 cloves garlic, crushed
- cooking oil spray

**1** Prepare a fire to glowing coals.

**2** Line a large frying pan or cast-iron camp oven with two pieces baking paper in opposite directions.

**3** Beat eggs in a large bowl. Add gnocchi, soup, cream, 1 cup of the Parmesan and the garlic; season. Stir gently to combine.

**4** Remove paper insert from the garlic bread; cut into 1.5cm slices. Pour gnocchi mixture into the pan; arrange garlic bread slices on top, overlapping slightly, sprinkle with remaining cheese. Spray with oil.

**5** Cook, uncovered, for 45 minutes until golden and set. Season to taste.

# BACON & CORN CHOWDER WITH GARLIC BREAD DIPPERS

RECIPE SERVES 4

PREP & COOK TIME 30 MINS

IN THE CAMP OVEN

## FIVE INGREDIENTS

300g diced bacon

2 green onions, sliced thinly, plus extra to serve

2 x 400g cans creamed corn

2 medium potatoes (400g), peeled, chopped into 2cm chunks

4 long bread rolls (560g), halved lengthways

## STAPLES

¼ cup (60ml) olive oil

1 tbsp plain flour (optional, see tips)

3 cloves garlic, crushed

1 chicken stock cube

**1** Heat 1 tablespoon of the oil in a camp oven or large saucepan over medium heat. Cook bacon for 5 minutes or until golden. Add green onion, flour (if using) and two-thirds of the garlic to the pan; cook, stirring, for 2 minutes or until fragrant.

**2** Add creamed corn, potato, stock cube and 2 cups (500ml) water; bring to a simmer and cook, covered, stirring frequently, for 15 minutes or until potato is tender. Season to taste.

**3** Meanwhile, preheat a grill plate (or barbecue). Place bread, remaining oil and garlic in a medium bowl; toss to coat. Season. Cook on grill plate for 1 minute each side or until char marks appear.

**4** Divide chowder among bowls or individual camping pans; top with extra green onion. Serve with garlic bread dippers.

***tips*** *The flour can be omitted if unavailable. The soup will be a little thinner but will still be delicious. Bread can also be toasted in a dry frying pan.*

# SMOKY WHITE BEAN STEW

RECIPE SERVES 6

PREP & COOK TIME
1 HOUR 15 MINS

IN THE CAMP OVEN

## FIVE INGREDIENTS

600g stale sourdough loaf, torn into small pieces

6 small chorizo (600g), halved lengthways

4 x 400g cans cannellini beans, drained

3 slices lemon

3 dried bay leaves

## STAPLES

¾ cup (180ml) olive oil

1 large red onion (300g), cut into 1cm wedges

5 cloves garlic, whole, bruised

2 tbsp sugar

**1** Prepare a fire to glowing coals.

**2** Toss bread with ½ cup (125ml) oil in a large bowl; season. Heat a large camp oven or deep skillet over medium-high heat. Once heated, add half the bread. Toss continuously for 4 minutes or until golden brown; transfer to a bowl. Repeat cooking with remaining bread. Reserve pan.

**3** To make the bean stew, wipe out reserved pan and return to the heat. Heat remaining oil; cook chorizo, turning occasionally for 5 minutes or until browned; remove from pan. Add onions and garlic; cook, stirring, for 5 minutes or until soft and lightly coloured.

**4** Stir in beans, lemon slices, bay leaves, sugar and 3 cups (750ml) of water. Bring to the boil then reduce to a simmer. Cook for 40 minutes or until the liquid has reduced by two-thirds and stew has thickened. Return chorizo to pan. Season to taste.

**5** Serve bean stew topped with fried bread.

# DAN DAN NOODLES

RECIPE SERVES 4

PREP & COOK TIME 20 MINS

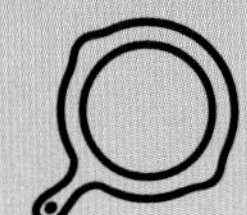

IN THE SKILLET

## FIVE INGREDIENTS

500g minced pork

⅓ cup (95g) hoisin sauce

300g dried egg noodles

400g broccolini, thick stems halved lengthways

chilli oil, to serve

## STAPLES

2 tbsp peanut butter

2 tbsp soy sauce

1 clove garlic, crushed

1 tbsp oil of choice

**1** Bring a large saucepan of salted water to the boil.

**2** Place 2 teaspoons peanut butter, 2 teaspoons soy sauce and a quarter of the garlic in each serving bowl.

**3** Heat oil in a large skillet or frying pan over high heat; cook mince, breaking it up with a spoon, for 8 minutes or until browned. Add hoisin sauce; cook for 1 minute or until caramelised.

**4** Meanwhile, cook noodles and broccolini in a saucepan of boiling water for 3 minutes or until cooked through. Ladle ⅓ cup (80ml) noodle cooking water into each serving bowl, then drain noodles.

**5** Stir peanut mixture and noodle cooking water in each bowl to combine. Top with noodles, pork, broccolini and chilli oil. Toss well before eating.

***tip*** *Broccolini can be substituted with buk choy, green beans or baby spinach leaves.*

PHILTER

# KANGAROO & ALE STEW

RECIPE SERVES 6

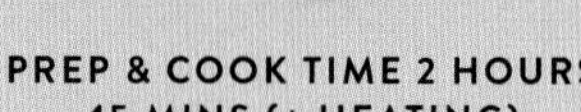

PREP & COOK TIME 2 HOURS 45 MINS (+ HEATING)

IN THE CAMP OVEN

## FIVE INGREDIENTS

- 1.5kg kangaroo, beef or lamb fillet, cut into 4cm pieces
- 460g packet cheese and chive scone mix
- 440ml can Guinness or stout
- 3 medium carrots (360g), chopped

## STAPLES

- ¼ cup (60ml) oil of choice
- 2 medium onions (300g), sliced thinly
- 3 cloves garlic, sliced thinly
- 2 tsp dried mixed herbs or oregano
- 1 tbsp sugar
- 2 beef or chicken stock cubes

1 Prepare a fire to glowing coals. Preheat a large camp oven with the lid on, over medium-high heat.

2 Meanwhile, toss kangaroo and 2 tablespoons of the scone mix in a large bowl. Season to taste.

3 Add 1 tablespoon of oil and half the kangaroo to camp oven; cook, turning, until browned. Transfer to a plate. Repeat with 1 tablespoon oil and remaining kangaroo.

4 Add remaining oil and the onion to oven; stir for 3 minutes or until softened. Add garlic and herbs; stir for 1 minute until fragrant. Add Guinness and sugar; bring to a simmer.

5 Return meat to oven with stock cubes and 3 cups (750ml) water; cover with the lid. Bring to a simmer. Spread coals out to reduce heat to low. Elevate camp oven to hang about 5cm over coals, then cover lid with coals. Cook, covered, for 2 hours, stirring halfway or until meat is just tender. If meat needs further cooking, reduce the distance between the oven and coals, and replace coals on the lid more frequently.

6 Meanwhile, place remaining scone mixture in a medium bowl; gradually stir in ¾ cup (180ml) water until combined.

7 Remove coals and lid from oven; stir in carrot, then cover stew with heaped tablespoons of scone mixture. Replace oven lid, cover with hot coals; cook for a further 20 minutes or until dumplings are risen and cooked through.

# INSTANT TONKOTSU-STYLE RAMEN

RECIPE SERVES 4

PREP & COOK TIME 25 MINS

IN A BILLY CAN

## FIVE INGREDIENTS

- 4 x 120g packets instant ramen
- 420g can sweetcorn, drained
- 225g can bamboo shoots, drained
- 2 green onions, sliced thinly
- 5g packet roasted seaweed snack sheets

## STAPLES

- 8 eggs
- ⅓ cup (100g) Japanese (Kewpie) mayonnaise
- 2 cloves garlic, crushed

**1** To soft-boil eggs, fill a billy can or large saucepan with 1.75 litres (7 cups) water; bring to the boil. Add four eggs; cook for 6 minutes. Using a slotted spoon, transfer eggs to a bowl of cold water; set aside. Reserve billy of boiling water.

**2** Meanwhile, place 1 tablespoon mayonnaise, ramen seasoning, a remaining raw egg and a quarter of the garlic into each serving bowl. Using a fork (or chopsticks), whisk until smooth.

**3** Cook ramen noodles in reserved boiling water for 4 minutes or until just cooked. Remove from heat. Pour 1½ cups (375ml) cooking water into each bowl; stir until smooth. Divide noodles among bowls.

**4** Drain and peel soft-boiled eggs; cut in half. Divide sweetcorn, bamboo shoots, eggs and green onion evenly among bowls. Serve with seaweed.

***tip*** *Japanese mayonnaise can be substituted with regular mayonnaise. Bamboo shoots can be substituted with canned water chestnuts or beansprouts.*

# SHRIMP BOIL

RECIPE SERVES 6

PREP & COOK TIME 35 MINS

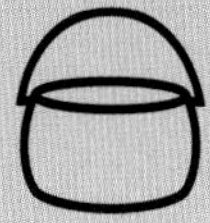

IN A BILLY CAN

## FIVE INGREDIENTS

2 tbsp Old Bay seasoning (see tips)

4 corn cobs (1kg), husks and silks removed

1kg baby red potatoes, halved

400g Cheese Kranksy chipolatas

1kg large raw prawns, unpeeled

## STAPLES

2 chicken or vegetable stock cubes

6 cloves garlic, peeled

200g butter, chopped

**1** Fill a billy can or large saucepan with 3 litres (12 cups) water. Add 1½ tablespoons Old Bay seasoning, the stock cubes and half the garlic; cover and bring to the boil.

**2** Meanwhile, cut cobs into thirds. Crush remaining garlic.

**3** Add potatoes to the billy; cook for 6 minutes or until just tender. Add corn and chipolatas; cook for 5 minutes. Add prawns; cook for 2 minutes or until just cooked through. Reserve 1 cup (250ml) cooking liquid; drain.

**4** To make shrimp boil sauce, place reserved cooking liquid in a small saucepan with the butter and crushed garlic; bring to a simmer. Cook, whisking occasionally, for 3 minutes or until emulsified. Season to taste.

**5** Line a table with newspaper (see tips). Using tongs, arrange shrimp boil on paper. Pour over a little sauce and sprinkle with remaining ½ teaspoon Old Bay seasoning. Serve with remaining sauce on the side.

***tips*** *You will need some newspaper but could also use baking paper. Prawns can be swapped with other seafood such as pipis, crab or squid; adjust cooking time accordingly. Old Bay seasoning (see glossary page 159) is available from selected supermarkets or can be swapped for a 35g sachet taco seasoning.*

# GNOCCHI & PUMPKIN CACIO E PEPE

RECIPE SERVES 4

PREP & COOK TIME 25 MINS

IN THE CAMP OVEN

## FIVE INGREDIENTS

- 400g Kent pumpkin, peeled, seeded, cut into a 1cm dice
- 2 x 500g packets gnocchi
- 1 bunch kale (400g), stems removed, torn coarsely
- 2 tbsp lemon juice
- 2 cups (160g) finely grated Parmesan

## STAPLES

- 2 tbsp olive oil
- 120g butter, chopped
- 1 tbsp freshly ground black pepper

**1** Heat oil in a large camp oven or saucepan over medium-high heat; cook pumpkin, turning for 8 minutes or until golden. Transfer to a plate, cover to keep warm.

**2** Fill same pan with water and season with salt (it's not necessary to clean it); bring to the boil over medium heat. Cook gnocchi and kale for 3 minutes or until tender. Reserve 1 cup (250ml) cooking water; drain well.

**3** To make the sauce, place butter and black pepper in a large frying pan over medium heat; cook for 1 minute or until pepper is fragrant. Add drained gnocchi mixture, lemon juice and reserved cooking water; stir vigorously to emulsify.

**4** Remove pan from the heat. Sprinkle over Parmesan; stand for 1 minute then stir vigorously again until the sauce is smooth. Stir in pumpkin and season to taste. Serve immediately.

NEW

# NACHOS IN A BAG

RECIPE SERVES 6

PREP & COOK TIME 15 MINS

IN THE SKILLET

## FIVE INGREDIENTS

- 500g beef mince
- 35g packet taco seasoning
- 175g packet flavoured corn chips (see tips)
- 1 cup (120g) grated cheddar
- guacamole, to serve

## STAPLES

- 1 tbsp oil of choice
- hot sauce, to serve

**1** Heat oil in a large frying pan over medium-high heat; cook mince, breaking it up with a spoon, for 8 minutes or until browned. Add taco seasoning; cook, stirring, for 2 minutes or until fragrant.

**2** Meanwhile, place the corn chip packet flat. Using scissors, cut down the centre of the long side of the packet to open.

**3** Top chips with cheddar, beef, guacamole and hot sauce.

***tips*** *You can also make individual nachos bags using 6 x 28g packets flavoured corn chips, cutting the top of the packets and dividing the toppings among the bags. Serve with salsa instead of the guacamole, if preferrred.*

# AL PASTOR CHICKEN SKEWERS

RECIPE SERVES 4

PREP + COOK TIME
20 MINS (+ STANDING)

ON THE GRILL

## FIVE INGREDIENTS

- 2 x 440g cans pineapple pieces in natural juice
- 1kg chicken thigh fillets, cut into 3cm pieces
- 35g sachet Mexican chilli spice mix
- 280g packet white corn tortillas
- ½ cup (150g) sriracha mayonnaise

## STAPLES

- 2 tbsp smoked paprika
- ½ cup (125ml) olive oil
- 1 small red onion (100g), sliced thinly
- 2 tbsp red wine vinegar

1 Heat a lidded barbecue with a flat plate to medium-high heat. Soak 8 wooden skewers in water (if not using metal skewers) for 15 minutes; drain.

2 Meanwhile, reserve ¼ cup (60ml) pineapple juice; drain remaining juice. Place juice, three-quarters of the pineapple, the chicken, spice mix, paprika and oil in a large zip-lock bag; season. Seal bag and massage chicken to combine; place in a cooler to marinate for 20 minutes.

3 To make the pineapple salsa, combine pineapple, onion and vinegar in a bowl; season to taste. Set aside to pickle.

4 Thread alternating pieces of marinated chicken and pineapple onto each skewer. Wrap tortillas in foil.

5 Cook skewers on barbecue flat plate for 7 minutes or until charred on one side. Turn skewers and add tortillas to flat plate; close barbecue lid. Cook for another 7 minutes or until chicken is charred and cooked through, and tortillas are warmed.

6 Remove chicken from skewers. Serve chicken on warmed tortillas with pineapple salsa and sriracha mayonnaise.

FRONT
CENTRE

# MISO & APPLE GLAZED PORK RIBS

RECIPE SERVES 4

PREP & COOK TIME
55 MINS (+ HEATING)

ON THE GRILL

## FIVE INGREDIENTS

- 1.5kg American-style pork ribs
- ⅓ cup (80g) white (shiro) miso paste
- ⅓ cup (80ml) long-life apple juice

## STAPLES

- 2 tbsp soy sauce
- ⅓ cup (75g) sugar
- 3 cloves garlic, crushed
- 1 tsp chilli flakes (optional)

**1** Bring a large saucepan of water to the boil. Add ribs, reduce heat to medium and bring to a simmer. Cover and cook for 35 minutes or until tender. Drain; transfer ribs to a tray.

**2** Meanwhile, preheat barbecue to low or prepare a fire to glowing coals.

**3** To make the glaze, in the same saucepan, combine miso, apple juice, soy sauce, sugar, garlic and chilli flakes (if using). Place saucepan over medium-high heat; cook for 5 minutes or until glaze has thickened slightly. Return ribs to the pan; turn to coat.

**4** Transfer ribs to barbecue and cook, turning halfway, for 10 minutes or until lightly charred, brushing occasionally with remaining glaze.

***tip*** *Try serving the ribs with baked potatoes or slaw and lime wedges.*

# EMBER-BAKED POTATOES WITH BABA GANOUSH

RECIPE SERVES 4

PREP & COOK TIME
50 MINS (+ HEATING)

IN THE FIRE

## FIVE INGREDIENTS

- 4 large orange sweet potatoes (1.2kg), scrubbed
- 2 large eggplant (1kg) or 6 medium zucchini (900g)
- 2 tbsp hulled tahini
- 2 tbsp lemon juice
- 1 tsp ground cumin, plus extra to serve

## STAPLES

- ¼ cup (60ml) olive oil, plus extra to serve
- 1 tsp salt
- 1 clove garlic, crushed
- chilli flakes, to serve

**1** Prepare a fire to glowing coals.

**2** Grease four x 30cm pieces of foil. Pierce potatoes all over with a fork. Rub each potato with 2 teaspoons of the oil and ¼ teaspoon salt. Place a potato in each foil piece; wrap tightly.

**3** Place potatoes around the edge of the fire; cook, turning occasionally for 45 minutes or until tender.

**4** Place eggplant or zucchini directly in embers around the edge of the fire; cook, turning occasionally, for 25 minutes or until completely soft in the centre. Using tongs, carefully remove eggplant or zucchini from the fire; brush off any embers and set aside to cool slightly. (Do not drain juices.)

**5** Meanwhile, place tahini, lemon juice, cumin, garlic and remaining oil in a medium bowl; stir until smooth. Slice eggplant or zucchini in half lengthways. Scoop flesh into the bowl; discard charred skin. Using a potato masher or fork, mash until well combined; season to taste.

**6** Slice sweet potatoes open lengthways; top with baba ganoush, extra oil, cumin and chilli flakes (if using).

***tip*** *Ground cumin can be replaced with sweet or smoked paprika.*

# EGGPLANT PARMI

RECIPE SERVES 4

PREP & COOK TIME
30 MINS (+ HEATING)

ON THE GRILL

## FIVE INGREDIENTS

- 2 large eggplants (1kg), halved lengthways
- 2 x 200g packets sliced leg ham
- 400g jar pasta sauce
- 1½ cups (150g) shredded mozzarella
- 2 Turkish bread rolls (200g), halved lengthways

## STAPLES

- cooking oil spray

1 Preheat a barbecue to low heat or prepare a fire to glowing coals.

2 Spray eggplant with oil and place, flesh-side down, on the barbecue or grate; cook, turning halfway, for 15 minutes or until just cooked through. Transfer, skin-side down, to a chopping board.

3 Using a spoon, scrape off any charred flesh. Divide ham, pasta sauce and mozzarella between eggplant halves. Return to the barbecue or fire; cook for 3 minutes or until cheese is melted and bubbling. Season well.

4 Meanwhile, spray bread with oil. Cook on barbecue or grate for 1 minute on each side or until toasted.

5 Serve toasted bread topped with eggplant parmi.

# MEDITERRANEAN FISH PARCELS

RECIPE SERVES 4

PREP & COOK TIME
25 MINS (+ HEATING)

IN THE FIRE

## FIVE INGREDIENTS

260g jar chargrilled capsicum in oil

2 medium lemons (280g), sliced thinly

2 x sides of snapper (500g each), skinless

500g mixed cherry tomatoes, halved

½ cup (75g) pitted mixed olives, halved

## STAPLES

2 cloves garlic, sliced thinly

**1** Prepare a fire to glowing coals. Reserve ¼ cup (60ml) of the chargrilled capsicum oil; drain remaining oil. Thinly slice capsicum.

**2** Place two x 80cm pieces of foil on a clean work surface. Drizzle each piece of foil with 2 teaspoons of the capsicum oil. Arrange lemon slices in the centre of each; top with a side of snapper. Arrange sliced capsicum, tomatoes, olives and garlic over each piece of fish. Drizzle with remaining capsicum oil; season to taste.

**3** Gather the edges of foil and fold into a parcel, twisting edges to seal.

**4** Cook parcels on the edge of glowing coals for 7 minutes on each side or until just cooked through.

***tips*** *You can use any seafood, or combination of, in these parcels, simply adjust the cooking time for the volume and thickness of the seafood. If you have fresh parsley or thyme, or mixed dried herbs on hand, scatter over when serving.*

# CHEESY MEATBALL TOMATO PASTA SOUP

RECIPE SERVES 4

PREP & COOK TIME 25 MINS

IN THE CAMP OVEN

### FIVE INGREDIENTS

500g pre-made meatballs (see tips)

250g small pasta shells

1.2 litres canned tomato soup

150g grated pizza cheese

⅓ cup (90g) basil pesto

### STAPLES

1 tbsp olive oil

**1** Heat oil in a large camp oven over medium-high heat. Cook meatballs, turning occasionally, for 5 minutes or until browned; remove and set aside.

**2** Add 2 cups (500ml) water to pan, scraping the base with a spoon to release flavour from the base. Bring to the boil. Add pasta; cook, stirring frequently, for 5 minutes.

**3** Add tomato soup and return meatballs with any resting juices to pan. Bring to a simmer then reduce heat to medium. Cook for 10 minutes or until pasta is al dente. Add extra water, ½ cup (125ml) at a time for a thinner consistency.

**4** Serve soup topped with cheese and pesto.

***tips*** *We used beef meatballs, however you can use lamb, chicken or pork, if preferred. If you are a fan of chilli you can add a sprinkling of chilli flakes to serve.*

# CAMPFIRE CHEESE BURGER PIZZA

RECIPE SERVES 4

PREP & COOK TIME
30 MINS (+ HEATING)

IN THE SKILLET

## FIVE INGREDIENTS

2 x 200g pre-made refrigerated pizza dough

4 beef burger patties (450g)

1 cup (260g) pizza sauce

6 burger cheese slices (60g), halved diagonally

12 burger crinkle-cut pickle slices

## STAPLES

2 tsp olive oil

cooking oil spray

sauce of choice, to serve

1 Prepare a fire to glowing coals or preheat a barbecue to medium-high heat. Bring dough to room temperature according to packet instructions.

2 Meanwhile, divide each burger patty into 3 to make 12 mini burger patties.

3 Heat oil in a large 25cm cast-iron skillet pan over medium-high heat. Cook patties for 5 minutes, turning halfway, or until golden and just cooked; transfer to a plate. Wipe pan clean and set aside to cool slightly.

4 Place one dough ball onto a large piece of baking paper. Using your fingertips, carefully stretch the dough into a 25cm round. Carefully invert dough into skillet to cover the base; remove baking paper.

5 Spread over half the pizza sauce, leaving a 1.5cm border. Top with half the patties. Place half a cheese slice over each patty and spray dough edges with oil.

6 Reduce pan heat to low-medium. Cover pan with a lid. Cook pizza for 10 minutes or until base is golden and cheese melts. Repeat with remaining dough and toppings.

7 Serve pizzas topped with pickles and sauce of choice.

RIGHT

# JAPANESE-STYLE FRIED RICE

RECIPE SERVES 4

PREP & COOK TIME
20 MINS (+ SOAKING)

IN THE SKILLET

## FIVE INGREDIENTS

- 40g sliced dried shiitake mushrooms
- 2 x 450g packets microwave long-grain rice
- 2 x 300g cans corn kernels, drained
- 150ml teriyaki sauce
- furikake seasoning, to sprinkle

## STAPLES

- 2 tbsp vegetable oil
- 4 eggs
- 2 tsp white vinegar
- sriracha or other chilli sauce, to serve

**1** Place mushrooms in large bowl; top with 2 cups (500ml) boiling water then cover. Set aside to soak for 30 minutes. Drain mushroom water into a large cast-iron frying pan or skillet. Coarsely chop mushrooms.

**2** Add mushrooms to soaking liquid in pan; place pan over medium-high heat and bring to the boil. Cook for 8 minutes or until water has evaporated. Add 1 tablespoon oil to mushrooms; cook for 2 minutes or until golden.

**3** Add remaining oil to mushrooms. To one side of the pan add rice, to the other side crack in eggs; cook, slowly mixing together, for 5 minutes or until rice is heated through and eggs are cooked.

**4** Add corn, teriyaki sauce and vinegar to pan; cook for 2 minutes or until well combined.

**5** Serve rice topped with furikake seasoning and sriracha.

# LENTIL SLOPPY JOES

RECIPE SERVES 4

PREP & COOK TIME 15 MINS

IN THE SKILLET

## FIVE INGREDIENTS

300g pre-chopped vegetable medley (see tips)

2 x 400g cans brown lentils, drained

2 x 400g jars pasta sauce (see tips)

4 damper rolls (270g), halved

75g Parmesan, shaved

## STAPLES

1 tbsp olive oil, plus extra to drizzle

**1** Heat oil in a saucepan over medium-high heat. Cook vegetables for 2 minutes; add lentils and pasta sauce. Cook for 5 minutes, stirring occasionally, until heated through. Season to taste.

**2** Meanwhile, heat a large frying pan or skillet over medium-high heat. Toast cut-side of rolls for 1 minute or until golden.

**3** To serve, fill rolls with lentil mixture and top with Parmesan, then drizzle with a little extra oil.

***tips*** *We used a supermarket vegetable medley mix of broccoli florets and carrot sticks. You can use any combination of stir-fry-style vegetables. Use either Napoletana or, for a chilli hit, arrabbiata pasta sauce.*

PRIMUS

# FIRE-ROASTED CHEESY PUMPKIN WEDGES

RECIPE SERVES 8

PREP & COOK TIME
1 HOUR 15 MINS (+ HEATING)

IN THE FIRE

## FIVE INGREDIENTS

2.5kg Kent pumpkin

2 tbsp harissa paste

350g tub prepared tabbouleh with mixed grains salad

½ cup (75g) seed mix

600g triple-cream brie, cut into 8 wedges

## STAPLES

⅓ cup (80ml) olive oil

**1** Prepare a fire to glowing coals.

**2** Cut pumpkin into eight wedges, then using a metal spoon, scoop out the seeds. Combine harissa paste, oil and salt to taste in a small bowl.

**3** Place each pumpkin wedge onto a separate sheet of greased foil. Reserve half the harrisa oil; brush each piece of pumpkin with remaining harissa oil. Wrap each pumpkin piece in the foil tightly.

**4** Place pumpkin at the edge of the hot coals; cook for 1 hour, turning halfway, or until pumpkin is tender when pierced with a thin bladed knife.

**5** Transfer pumpkin parcels to a large frying pan or skillet. Using tongs, carefully open each parcel; top with combined tabbouleh and seed mixture, and a wedge of brie. Place skillet over a medium heat, covered with a lid; cook for 15 minutes or until cheese melts.

**6** Serve roast pumpkin wedges drizzled with reserved harissa oil.

# OUTDOOR DESSERTS

# SPEEDY UPSIDE-DOWN PINEAPPLE CAKE

RECIPE SERVES 6 PREP & COOK TIME 20 MINS ON THE GRILL

## FIVE INGREDIENTS

230g unfilled round sponge cake

½ cup (175g) golden syrup, plus extra to serve

440g can pineapple slices in syrup, drained

custard, to serve (optional)

## STAPLES

cooking oil spray

1 Preheat a barbecue to medium heat. Pierce top of sponge all over with a fork.

2 Lay a 50cm length of foil on a flat surface, top with a second 50cm length of foil in the opposite direction to create a cross shape; spray generously with cooking oil. Pour golden syrup into the centre of the foil, spread to form a round shape the same size as the sponge. Top with pineapple slices, in a single layer, then place cake, top-side down, over pineapple. Bring foil up and wrap around cake; secure tightly.

3 Place cake, pineapple-side down on barbecue; cook, covered, for 15 minutes or until pineapple is lightly charred. Carefully open foil parcel and flip cake onto a plate; drizzle with extra golden syrup. Serve with custard, if you like.

***tip*** *The pineapple cake can also be cooked in a cast-iron camp oven over an open fire or in a large frying pan with a lid.*

# CAMPFIRE ORANGE BROWNIES

RECIPE SERVES 8

PREP & COOK TIME
40 MINS (+ HEATING)

IN THE FIRE

### FIVE INGREDIENTS

8 medium oranges (1.9kg)

380g packet brownie mix

caramel sauce, to serve

### STAPLES

⅓ cup (80ml) vegetable oil

2 eggs

**1** Prepare a fire to glowing coals.

**2** Using a small sharp knife, cut 2cm from the top of each orange to create a lid; reserve. Cut around the inside edge of the flesh of the orange to release it. Using a spoon, scoop inside the skin to remove the orange flesh, creating a hollow orange skin. Reserve orange flesh for another use (see tips).

**3** Combine brownie mix, oil and eggs in a large bowl. Divide brownie mix evenly among orange shells (about 2-3 tablespoons per orange); top with orange lids.

**4** Wrap each orange in two layers of foil to enclose. Place in embers around the edge of the fire or over glowing coals; cook, rotating occasionally, for 25 minutes or until brownie is fudgy. Carefully open foil parcels and serve drizzled with caramel sauce.

***tips*** *You could eat the orange flesh while you wait for the brownies to cook, or keep it to have for breakfast the next day. The cooking time will vary depending on the heat of the embers or coals.*

# CINNAMON ROLL-UPS

RECIPE MAKES 6

PREP & COOK TIME
25 MINS (+ HEATING)

IN THE SKILLET

## FIVE INGREDIENTS

- 1 tbsp cinnamon sugar
- 2 x 200g pre-made refrigerated pizza dough
- 2 tbsp finely chopped pistachios
- chocolate custard, to serve

## STAPLES

- 80g butter, softened, plus extra to grease
- plain flour, to dust

**1** Prepare a fire to glowing coals.

**2** Heat a large cast-iron skillet over the fire for 5 minutes or until medium hot. Combine butter and 2 teaspoons of the cinnnamon sugar in a small bowl.

**3** On a lightly floured piece of baking paper, roll one portion of pizza dough into an 18cm x 26cm rectangle. Spread half the cinnamon butter mixture over the dough; sprinkle with half the pistachios. Roll the dough up tightly from the long side to form a log. Using a sharp knife, cut the log into 9 even pieces. Repeat with remaining dough, cinnamon butter mixture and pistachios.

**4** Thread three dough rounds onto each skewer to make six skewers in total.

**5** Add extra butter to the hot pan; swirl to grease base. In batches, add scroll skewers to pan; cook for 4 minutes each side or until golden brown. Repeat with remaining skewers.

**6** Sprinkle scrolls with extra cinnamon sugar and serve with chocolate custard.

***tip*** *If you don't have a rolling pin use a wine bottle to roll out the dough instead.*

# DOS LECHES TIN CAKES

RECIPE MAKES 4

PREP & COOK TIME
1 HOUR (+ HEATING)

IN THE CAMP OVEN

## FIVE INGREDIENTS

- 4 x 270ml cans coconut milk
- 540g vanilla cake mix with frosting
- 170g tube condensed milk
- 2 tbsp underproof rum (optional)
- ¼ cup (10g) toasted coconut flakes

## STAPLES

- 100ml vegetable oil
- 3 eggs
- 1 tsp salt

**1** Prepare a fire to glowing coals.

**2** Meanwhile, empty the cans of coconut milk into a large bowl and set aside.

**3** To prepare the tins, remove the labels, rinse and dry, taking care of sharp edges. Add 1 tsp of vegetable oil to each tin and carefully grease with paper towel.

**4** Combine cake mix, eggs, remaining oil and 1 cup (250ml) of the coconut milk in another large bowl.

**5** Fill the tins three-quarters full with cake batter (around 1 cup/200g batter). Place tins in a camp oven or lidded flameproof casserole dish. Place camp oven close to coals; cook for 40 minutes or until a wooden skewer inserted into the centre of a cake comes out clean.

**6** Meanwhile, add condensed milk, rum (if using) and salt to the remaining coconut milk; stir to combine. Using a wooden skewer, poke multiple deep holes into the cakes. Carefully and slowly pour coconut milk mixture over cakes (see tip).

**7** Top cakes with ready-made frosting and coconut flakes.

***tip*** *You will have coconut milk mixture left over. Serve along with cakes, or reserve and pour over warm damper or pancakes.*

# APRICOT CAMP CROSTATA

RECIPE SERVES 4

PREP & COOK TIME
35 MINS (+ HEATING)

IN THE SKILLET

## FIVE INGREDIENTS

375g packet pastry mix

1 cup (120g) almond meal

1 tsp ground ginger

1 cup (320g) apricot jam

¼ cup (20g) flaked almonds

## STAPLES

½ cup (110g) caster sugar, plus extra to sprinkle

60g unsalted butter, softened

¼ cup (35g) plain flour

**1** Prepare a fire to glowing coals.

**2** Meanwhile, prepare pastry according to packet instructions, using ¼ cup (55g) of the sugar and ½ cup (125ml) water.

**3** Transfer dough to a large piece of baking paper on a flat surface. Rest for 5 minutes.

**4** Meanwhile, in the same bowl, place butter, flour, almond meal, remaining ¼ cup (55g) of the sugar and the ginger. Using your fingertips, rub mixture together until it resembles large breadcrumbs.

**5** Roll the dough out on baking paper into a 30cm round, about 5mm thick. Spread apricot jam over dough leaving a 3cm border. Fold the edges of the pastry in around the jam. Scatter over crumble mixture and almonds.

**6** Transfer crostata on the baking paper into a deep skillet or large camp oven. Bake propped up in hot coals for 20-30 minutes or until pastry and top are golden brown.

**7** Stand crostata for 20 minutes before sprinkling with extra sugar. Slice to serve.

***tip*** *The cooking time may vary depending on the heat from the coals. Check a few times throughout to avoid crostata from overcooking.*

# STROOPWAFFLE S'MORES

RECIPE MAKES 4

PREP & COOK TIME 10 MINS

IN THE FIRE

### FIVE INGREDIENTS

200g Nutella

8 (2 x 125g packets) stroopwaffles

16 jumbo marshmallows

**1** Spread Nutella over half of the stroopwaffles.

**2** Toast 2 marshmallows per skewer in the fire, rotating, until softened and charred.

**3** Sandwich a Nutella-covered stroopwaffle and a plain stroopwaffle together on either side of a marshmallow skewer; pull to release from skewer.

***tip*** *Heat Nutella gently in a small saucepan over low heat, if necessary.*

# COCONUT & CHOC-CHIP CAMPFIRE BRIOCHE LOAF

RECIPE SERVES 6-8

PREP & COOK TIME 15 MINS

IN THE SKILLET

## FIVE INGREDIENTS

2 cups (150g) unsweetened shredded coconut, toasted

395g can sweetened condensed milk

1 sliced brioche loaf with chocolate chips (500g)

## STAPLES

100g butter, melted

1 Heat a large cast-iron skillet or pan big enough to fit brioche loaf over a fire.

2 Meanwhile, combine toasted coconut, condensed milk and melted butter in a bowl. Spread about 2 tablespoons of the mixture onto each slice of brioche, keeping pieces together to make a loaf. Wrap tightly in foil.

3 Toast each side of the loaf, rotating in the pan or over the fire for 1 minute each side or until warm and toasted. Serve immediately.

***tip*** *You could also cook the loaf over the fire without a skillet, wrapped in heavy-duty barbecue foil that can withstand fire.*

# CHERRY APPLE COBBLER

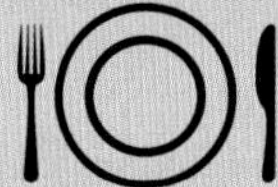

RECIPE SERVES 6-8

PREP & COOK TIME 45 MINS

IN THE CAMP OVEN

## FIVE INGREDIENTS

- 470g packet vanilla cake mix with icing mix
- 680g jar morello cherries
- 800g can apple pie fruit
- 250ml carton long-life cream
- ⅓ cup (25g) toasted coconut flakes

## STAPLES

- ¼ cup (60ml) long-life milk
- ¼ cup (60ml) oil
- 1 egg, beaten lightly

1 Combine cake mix, milk, oil and egg in a large bowl.

2 Drain off ¾ cup (180ml) liquid from morello cherries and discard. Place remaining liquid and morello cherries in a cast-iron camp oven. Stir in 2 tablespoons of the icing mixture and apple pie fruit. Place over medium heat and bring to a simmer.

3 Evenly spoon the cake batter over the cherry mixture to completely cover fruit. Cover with a tight-fitting lid. Cook for 15-20 minutes or until golden brown and a skewer inserted in the cake comes out clean.

4 Meanwhile, combine cream and ¼ of the remaining icing mixture.

5 Serve warm cobbler topped with sweetened cream and toasted coconut flakes.

# CHARRED MANGO WITH STRAWBERRY YOGHURT

RECIPE SERVES 6

PREP & COOK TIME 10 MINS

ON THE GRILL

## FIVE INGREDIENTS

6 small mangoes (1.8kg), halved either side of the stone

2 x 15g packets strawberry crisps (see tips)

1 cup (280g) vanilla yoghurt

2 tbsp chopped pistachios

## STAPLES

honey or maple syrup, to serve

**1** Heat an oiled grill plate (or grill or barbecue) over high heat; cook mango cheeks, cut-side down, for 5 minutes or until tender and char marks appear.

**2** Meanwhile, crumble one packet of the strawberry crisps into a small bowl.

**3** Divide yoghurt among each serving bowl. Top with mango cheeks, pistachios, crumbled and whole strawberry crisps. Drizzle with honey to serve.

***tips*** *Strawberry crisps are freeze dried strawberries without added sugar available in the snack section of supermarkets. They are great for camping. If mangoes are unavailable you can use other fruit such as peaches or plums, pineapple wedges (either fresh or canned), ripe pear halves or thick red apple slices instead.*

# HOKEY POKEY CAMP OVEN BROWNIE

RECIPE SERVES 4

PREP & COOK TIME 45 MINS (+ HEATING & COOLING)

IN THE CAMP OVEN

## FIVE INGREDIENTS

- 200g dark chocolate, chopped
- 1 cup (220g) firmly packed brown sugar
- 1 tsp baking powder
- 250g Cadbury Favourites, unwrapped, chopped coarsely

## STAPLES

- 125g butter, chopped or ½ cup (125ml) vegetable oil
- 2 eggs, beaten lightly
- 1 cup (150g) plain flour

**1** Prepare a fire to glowing coals.

**2** Line a lightly greased medium camp oven or deep skillet with lid with two sheets of baking paper, coming halfway up the side of the oven.

**3** Place butter (or oil) and dark chocolate in a medium saucepan; stir over low heat until almost smooth. Set aside to cool for 10 minutes.

**4** Add brown sugar and egg to chocolate mixture; stir until combined. Add sifted flour and baking powder (see tip); stir until just combined. Fold in half the chocolate pieces.

**5** Spread mixture into prepared oven and press in remaining chocolate pieces, then cover with lid. Elevate 10cm over glowing coals. Place coals on the lid. Cook for 30 minutes or until a skewer inserted in the centre comes out with moist crumbs, checking after 15 minutes and replacing hot coals on lid if needed. Remove from heat.

**6** Cool in pan for 10 minutes; remove and cool completely before cutting to serve.

***tip*** *In place of a sieve, stir flour and baking powder in a bowl with a whisk or fork to combine.*

# SKILLET SALTED GOLDEN SYRUP PUDDING

RECIPE SERVES 8

PREP & COOK TIME
45 MINS (+ HEATING)

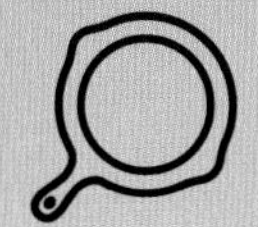

IN THE SKILLET

## FIVE INGREDIENTS

1 tbsp baking powder

½ tsp sea salt flakes, plus extra to serve

1 tsp vanilla bean paste

300ml long-life cream

200ml golden syrup

## STAPLES

1½ cups (225g) plain flour

¼ cup (55g) caster sugar

60g butter, chopped

225ml milk or long-life milk

**1** Prepare a fire to glowing coals.

**2** Lightly grease a 25cm deep cast-iron skillet.

**3** Combine flour, baking powder, sugar and salt in a large bowl. Using your fingertips, rub butter into flour mixture until mixture resembles fine breadcrumbs. Stir in milk and vanilla until combined. Spoon mixture into prepared pan. Set aside.

**4** Meanwhile, place long-life cream and golden syrup in a medium saucepan over medium heat. Bring to a simmer. Cook for 2 minutes. Remove from heat. Carefully pour mixture over batter.

**5** Place pan on grill over coals. Cover with foil or a lid. Cook for 30 minutes or until pudding is set or a skewer inserted into the centre comes out clean.

**6** Serve pudding warm sprinkled with extra sea salt flakes.

# CHEESECAKE CREAM WITH FIRE-ROASTED STRAWBERRIES

RECIPE SERVES 4

PREP & COOK TIME
15 MINS (+ HEATING)

IN THE SKILLET

### FIVE INGREDIENTS

- 250g tub Philadelphia classic cream cheese icing (see tips)
- 200g crème fraîche or sour cream
- 2 tsp finely grated lemon rind
- 500g strawberries, hulled, halved or quartered if large
- 6 Scottish shortbread biscuits, crushed (see tips)

### STAPLES

- 2 tbsp caster sugar

1 Prepare a fire to glowing coals.

2 Place cream cheese icing, crème fraîche and lemon rind in a bowl; whisk until combined and mixture is light.

3 Combine strawberries and sugar in a cast-iron skillet. Carefully sit skillet on the edge of glowing coals. Heat for 10 minutes or until strawberries just begin to release their juices.

4 To serve, divide cream cheese mixture among serving bowls. Top with hot strawberries and sprinkle with crushed biscuits.

***tips*** *You could also use soft spreadable cream cheese sweetened with either sugar, honey or maple syrup. Crush the shortbread biscuits by wrapping them in a clean tea towel or placing them in a zip-lock bag and hitting with the base of a pan – this gives a mixture of coarse and fine crumbs that works well in this recipe. This recipe is best made right before serving.*

# CAMPFIRE CINNAMON FRUIT PIES

RECIPE MAKES 4

PREP & COOK TIME
25 MINS (+ HEATING)

IN THE FIRE

## FIVE INGREDIENTS

8 slices cinnamon donut bread

700g jar fruit in juice (see tips), drained

1 tbsp cinnamon sugar, plus extra to sprinkle

1 litre (4 cups) long-life custard

⅓ cup (40g) pecans, chopped

## STAPLES

60g butter, softened

1 Prepare a fire to glowing coals.

2 Preheat a well-greased cast-iron jumbo double-hole jaffle iron (see tips) in fire. Butter both sides of bread slices. Working with two slices of bread at a time, place a slice of bread in each hole and press down with tongs to make an indentation. Fill each hole with 2-3 tablespoons fruit then scatter each with 1 teaspoon cinnamon sugar, and top each with another buttered piece of bread.

3 Place the jaffle iron right in the middle of the hottest part of the fire and hold (wearing gloves if hot) for 3 minutes, turning halfway through, or until bread is golden.

4 Remove jaffles from iron and sprinkle over extra cinnamon sugar; cover to keep warm. Repeat with remaining buttered bread, fruit and cinnamon sugar to make four jaffles in total.

5 Stand a few minutes before serving as the centres will be very hot. Spoon over custard and scatter with pecans.

***tips*** *You could use apricot halves, plums, peaches or pears for this recipe. We used an 11cm square double hole jaffle iron, available from camping shops. You could also use a single hole jaffle iron.*

REMOTE
PROJECTS AUSTRALIA
UTILITY GOODS DESIGNED IN BYRON BAY.
EXPLORE YOUR BACKYARD — AUSTRALIA
IS THE LAST FRONTIER.

# PEAR FRITTERS WITH BLUEBERRY SYRUP

RECIPE SERVES 4

PREP & COOK TIME 20 MINS

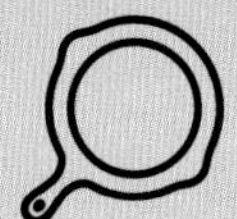

IN THE SKILLET

## FIVE INGREDIENTS

- 125g fresh blueberries
- 200g pancake mix (see tips)
- 4 medium firm pears (920g), peeled, sliced thickly lengthways
- ¾ cup (105g) salted caramel nuts, chopped coarsely

## STAPLES

- ⅓ cup (80ml) honey or maple syrup
- ¼ cup (60ml) vegetable oil

**1** Combine blueberries, honey and 2 tablespoons water in a small saucepan. Cook blueberries over medium-high heat, stirring occasionally, for 5 minutes or until syrupy and berries start to break down. Cover to keep warm; set aside.

**2** Prepare pancake mix according to packet instructions; pour into a small bowl.

**3** Heat 1 tablespoon of the oil in a large frying pan over medium heat.

**4** In batches, dip pear slices into the pancake batter; cook coated pear slices, adding more oil between batches, for 2 minutes each side or until golden. Drain on paper towel.

**5** Top fritters with blueberry syrup and salted caramel nuts to serve.

***tips*** *For ease, use a bottled pancake mix to mix and shake. Any leftover pancake batter can be refrigerated and used the following day for breakfast.*

# GLOSSARY

**ALMONDS** flat, pointy-tipped nuts with a pitted brown shell enclosing a creamy white kernel that is covered by a brown skin.
**meal** also known as ground almonds.
**BAKING POWDER** a raising agent consisting mainly of 2 parts cream of tartar to 1 part bicarbonate of soda.
**BEANS**
**cannellini** a small white bean similar in appearance and flavour to other white beans, all of which can be substituted for the other.
**green** also known as French or string beans, this long thin fresh bean is consumed in its entirety once cooked.
**BEETROOT** also known as red beets; firm, round root vegetable.
**BICARBONATE OF SODA** used as a leavening agent in baking.
**BREADCRUMBS, PANKO (JAPANESE)** available in two kinds: larger pieces and fine crumbs; have a lighter texture than Western-style ones.
**CHEESE**
**bocconcini** walnut-sized, baby mozzarella. Sold fresh, it will only keep, refrigerated in brine, 1 or 2 days at the most.
**cheddar** the most common cow's milk 'tasty' cheese; should be aged, hard and have a pronounced bite.
**cream** commonly called Philadelphia or Philly; a soft cow-milk cheese, its fat content ranges from 14% to 33%.
**gruyère** a hard-rind Swiss cheese with small holes and a nutty, slightly salty flavour.
**haloumi** a firm, cream-coloured sheep-milk cheese matured in brine; haloumi can be grilled or fried, briefly, without breaking down. Should be eaten while warm as it becomes rubbery on cooling.
**mozzarella** soft, spun-curd cheese; originating in southern Italy. Generally made from cow's milk, it is the most popular pizza cheese because of its low melting point and elasticity when heated.
**Parmesan** also called Parmigiano; is a hard, grainy cow-milk cheese originating in Italy. Reggiano is the best variety.
**pizza cheese** a commercial blend of varying proportions of processed grated mozzarella, cheddar and Parmesan.
**CHILLI**
**jalapeño** pronounced hah-lah-pain-yo. Fairly hot, medium-sized, plump, dark green chilli; available pickled, sold canned or bottled, and fresh, from greengrocers.
**oil** a condiment made from vegetable oil that has been infused with chilli. Different types of oil and chilli are used, and other ingredients may also be included. Commonly used in Asian cooking.
**CHOCOLATE, DARK** also called luxury chocolate; made of a high percentage of cocoa liquor and cocoa butter, and little added sugar.
**COCONUT**
**flaked** dried flaked coconut flesh.
**milk** not the liquid inside the fruit (coconut water), but the diluted liquid from the second pressing of the white flesh of a mature coconut.
**shredded** unsweetened thin strips of dried coconut flesh.
**CORIANDER** also known as pak chee or Chinese parsley; a bright-green leafy herb with a pungent flavour. Both stems and roots of coriander are also used in cooking; wash well before using. Also available ground or as seeds; these should not be substituted for fresh as the tastes are completely different.
**CREAM**
**sour** a thick, commercially-cultured sour cream with a minimum fat content of 35%.
**thickened** a whipping cream that contains a thickener. It has a minimum fat content of 35%.
**CRÈME FRAÎCHE** a mature, naturally fermented cream (minimum fat content 35%) with a slightly tangy, nutty flavour. Can be used in sweet and savoury dishes.
**CUSTARD POWDER** instant mixture used to make pouring custard; similar to North American instant pudding mixes.
**EGGPLANT** also known as aubergine. Ranges in size from tiny to very large and in colour from pale green to deep purple.

**FIVE SPICE POWDER** a fragrant mixture of ground cinnamon, cloves, star anise, Sichuan pepper and fennel seeds.

**FLOUR**

**plain** a general all-purpose wheat flour.

**self-raising** plain flour sifted with baking powder in the proportion of 1 cup flour to 2 teaspoons baking powder.

**GINGER, GROUND** also called powdered ginger; used as a flavouring in baking but cannot be substituted for fresh ginger.

**GOLDEN SYRUP** a by-product of refined sugarcane; pure maple syrup or honey can be substituted.

**HARISSA** a North African paste made from dried red chillies, garlic, olive oil and caraway seeds; can be used as a rub for meat, an ingredient in sauces and dressings, or as a condiment.

**HOISIN SAUCE** a thick, sweet and spicy Chinese barbecue sauce made from salted fermented soybeans, onions and garlic; used as a marinade or baste, or to accent stir-fries and barbecued or roasted foods.

**HONEY** the variety sold in a squeezable container is not suitable for the recipes in this book.

**MAPLE SYRUP** distilled from the sap of sugar maple trees found only in Canada and the USA. Maple-flavoured syrup or pancake syrup is not an adequate substitute for the real thing.

**MISO PASTE** fermented soybean paste. There are many types of miso, each with its own aroma, flavour, colour and texture; it can be kept, airtight, for up to a year in the fridge. Buy in tubs or plastic packs from most supermarkets.

**MUSHROOMS**

**field** large, flat mushrooms with a rich earthy flavour, ideal for filling and barbecuing.

**shiitake** when fresh are also known as Chinese black, forest or golden oak mushrooms. Large, meaty and, although cultivated, have the earthiness and taste of wild mushrooms. When dried, rehydrate in hot water before use.

**OIL**

**cooking spray** we use a cooking spray made from canola oil.

**olive** made from ripened olives. Extra virgin and virgin are the first and second press, respectively, of the olives; "light" refers to taste not fat levels.

**sesame** made from roasted, crushed, white sesame seeds; a flavouring rather than a cooking medium.

**vegetable** oils sourced from plant rather than animal fats.

**OLD BAY SEASONING** a blend of 18 different herbs and spices, including mustard, celery salt, black pepper, cinnamon, ginger, cayenne pepper, paprika and bay leaves. Originally created in Baltimore, Maryland.

**ONIONS, GREEN** also called, incorrectly, shallot; an immature onion picked before the bulb has formed. Has a long, bright-green edible stalk.

**PEPITAS** are the pale green kernels of dried pumpkin seeds.

**POLENTA** also known as cornmeal; a flour-like cereal made of dried corn (maize). Also the dish made from it.

**ROCKET** also called arugula and rucola; peppery green leaf eaten raw in salads or used in cooking. Baby leaves are smaller and less peppery.

**SOY SAUCE** made from fermented soybeans. We use Japanese soy sauce unless indicated otherwise.

**SUGAR**

**brown** very soft, finely granulated sugar retaining molasses for its characteristic colour and flavour.

**caster** finely granulated table sugar.

**TAHINI** sesame seed paste, available from Middle Eastern food stores and supermarkets.

**TOFU** also known as bean curd, an off-white, custard-like product made from the 'milk' of crushed soy beans; comes fresh as soft or firm. Leftover fresh tofu can be refrigerated in water (which is changed daily) for up to 4 days.

**VANILLA BEAN PASTE** made from vanilla beans and contains real seeds. Is highly concentrated: 1 teaspoon replaces a whole vanilla bean.

# CONVERSION CHART

## measures

One Australian metric measuring cup holds approximately 250ml; one Australian metric tablespoon holds 20ml; one Australian metric teaspoon holds 5ml.

The difference between one country's measuring cups and another's is within a two- or three-teaspoon variance, and will not affect your cooking results. North America, New Zealand and the United Kingdom use a 15ml tablespoon.

All cup and spoon measurements are level. The most accurate way of measuring dry ingredients is to weigh them. When measuring liquids, use a clear glass or plastic jug with the metric markings.

The imperial measurements used in these recipes are approximate only. Measurements for cake pans are approximate only. Using same-shaped cake pans of a similar size should not affect the outcome of your baking. We measure the inside top of the cake pan to determine sizes.

We use extra-large eggs with an average weight of 60g.

## dry measures

| metric | imperial |
|---|---|
| 15g | ½oz |
| 30g | 1oz |
| 60g | 2oz |
| 90g | 3oz |
| 125g | 4oz (¼lb) |
| 155g | 5oz |
| 185g | 6oz |
| 220g | 7oz |
| 250g | 8oz (½lb) |
| 280g | 9oz |
| 315g | 10oz |
| 345g | 11oz |
| 375g | 12oz (¾lb) |
| 410g | 13oz |
| 440g | 14oz |
| 470g | 15oz |
| 500g | 16oz (1lb) |
| 750g | 24oz (1½lb) |
| 1kg | 32oz (2lb) |

## oven temperatures

The oven temperatures in this book are for conventional ovens; if you have a fan-forced oven, decrease the temperature by 10-20 degrees.

| | °C (Celsius) | °F (Fahrenheit) |
|---|---|---|
| Very slow | 120 | 250 |
| Slow | 150 | 300 |
| Moderately slow | 160 | 325 |
| Moderate | 180 | 350 |
| Moderately hot | 200 | 400 |
| Hot | 220 | 425 |
| Very hot | 240 | 475 |

## liquid measures

| metric | imperial |
|---|---|
| 30ml | 1 fluid oz |
| 60ml | 2 fluid oz |
| 100ml | 3 fluid oz |
| 125ml | 4 fluid oz |
| 150ml | 5 fluid oz |
| 190ml | 6 fluid oz |
| 250ml | 8 fluid oz |
| 300ml | 10 fluid oz |
| 500ml | 16 fluid oz |
| 600ml | 20 fluid oz |
| 1000ml (1 litre) | 1¾ pints |

## length measures

| metric | imperial |
|---|---|
| 3mm | ⅛in |
| 6mm | ¼in |
| 1cm | ½in |
| 2cm | ¾in |
| 2.5cm | 1in |
| 5cm | 2in |
| 6cm | 2½in |
| 8cm | 3in |
| 10cm | 4in |
| 13cm | 5in |
| 15cm | 6in |
| 18cm | 7in |
| 20cm | 8in |
| 22cm | 9in |
| 25cm | 10in |
| 28cm | 11in |
| 30cm | 12in (1ft) |

# INDEX

# R



# S



# T



# V



# X



# Z

**PUBLISHED IN 2023 BY ARE MEDIA BOOKS, AUSTRALIA.**
**ARE MEDIA BOOKS IS A DIVISION OF ARE MEDIA PTY LTD.**

**Are Media**
**CHIEF EXECUTIVE OFFICER** Jane Huxley

**Are Media Books**
**GROUP PUBLISHER** Nicole Byers
**EDITORIAL & FOOD DIRECTOR** Sophia Young
**BOOKS DIRECTOR** David Scotto
**CREATIVE DIRECTOR** Hannah Blackmore
**MANAGING EDITOR** Stephanie Kistner
**EDITOR** Amanda Lees
**FOOD EDITOR** Sophia Young
**PRODUCTION CONTROLLER** Kara Stead

**RECIPE DEVELOPERS** Rebecca Lyall, Clare Maguire, Caitlyn McGrath, Olivia Andrews

**PHOTOGRAPHER** Luisa Brimble
**STYLIST** Olivia Blackmore
**PHOTOCHEFS** Sophia Young, Rebecca Lyall
**PHOTOCHEF ASSISTANT** Patrick Irving

**LIFESTYLE MODELS** Kelsie Walker, Patrick Irving, Elizabeth Fiduccia, Tamika O'Neill

**PRINTED IN CHINA**
by Leo Paper Products.

A catalogue record for this book is available from the National Library of Australia.
ISBN 978-1-76122-069-2 (paperback)



**PUBLISHED BY** Are Media Books,
a division of Are Media Pty Ltd,
54 Park St, Sydney; GPO Box 4088,
Sydney, NSW 2001, Australia
Ph +61 2 9282 8000
www.awwcookbooks.com.au

**INTERNATIONAL RIGHTS ENQUIRIES**
internationalrights@aremedia.com.au

**ORDER BOOKS**
Phone 1300 322 007 (within Australia)
or order online at
www.awwcookbooks.com.au

**RECIPE ENQUIRIES**
recipeenquiries@aremedia.com.au

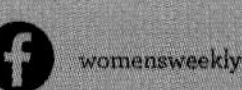